SURVIVOR'S REMORSE

GOOD NIGHT,
I'LL SEE YOU IN THE MORNING

SURVIVOR'S REMORSE

GOOD NIGHT,
I'LL SEE YOU IN THE MORNING

A Journey Through Grief, Love, and Redemption

by Elliott Norman, Sr.

Young Adult, Adult Non-Fiction
Grief Memoir

EQUIP PRESS

Colorado Springs

Survivor's Remorse: Goodnight I'll See You In The Morning

Copyright © 2025 Survivor's Remorse / Rev. Elliott S. Norman Sr.

First Edition: 2025

Survivor's Remorse / Rev. Elliott S. Norman Sr.

Paperback ISBN: 978-1-966923-13-8

ePUB ISBN: 978-1-966923-14-5

DEDICATION

*To my beloved wife of 48 years, whose love re-
mains my guiding light. In my grief and struggle,
I find strength in God's grace, and in His mercy.
I continue to carry your memory.*

*This book is a testament to the enduring power of
love, faith, and hope.*

With all my heart, I dedicate this to you.

Forever yours,

Elliott

FOREWARD

Losing someone you love is one of life's most profound and personal journeys. In this book, my father shares his intimate reflections on grief, faith, resilience, and the enduring power of love that binds a family in the most difficult of times. After forty-eight years together, the loss of my mother—his wife of nearly half a century—left an indelible mark on our lives. His honest words offer solace, understanding, and a reminder that even in the depths of sorrow God provides hope and healing. It is my hope that his story will resonate with others navigating similar paths, providing comfort and the reassurance that they are not alone. May this book serve as a testament to the strength of love, the enduring spirit of those who grieve, and God's grace.

With love and compassion,

Dr. Ardra Norman Gilchrist

TABLE OF CONTENTS

ACKNOWLEDGEMENTS

I would like to sincerely thank my family and friends for their unwavering support and love throughout this journey. Your kindness and understanding have been a guiding light in the darkest times. I am deeply grateful to the members of Clifford Memorial Presbyterian Church in Grovetown, Georgia, for their comfort, prayers, and fellowship. Your compassion has meant more than words can express.

Introduction

After my wife's death on March 14, 2025 I found myself experiencing emotions that were (to me) new and different: emotions associated with grief. Specifically, emotions that are associated with denial, anger, bargaining, depression, and acceptance. I did not know what to do. I tried rationalization. I prayed constantly. However, the moment I let my guard down thoughts would creep back into my mind summoning the emotions of grief. I started writing this book as a cathartic antidote to those emotions. I write this book not from an intellectual perspective but from my raw emotions. I write it not as a blueprint for what others ought to do but to show others what helped me. This book is an intimate and raw opening to the journey of grief and questioning after losing a loved one.

It tells the story of my first introduction to death through a vision. This story reveals how I have had to face the death of many loved ones, including my grandmother, and how those deaths impacted me. Yet, nothing I have ever experienced prepared me for the death of my wife. I take the reader on my journey through illness and loss. I recount the events leading to my wife's death. I share my moments of strength, weakness, love, and grief. I share my attempt to navigate isolation and an emotional void.

Readers are introduced to what I have termed *the healing breath:* the unconscious use of inspirational breathing as a coping mechanism. Together we explore how death causes us to question the nature of love and the depth of the bond shared with the deceased. Together we examine how in survivor's remorse we question whether we should love if it will cause so much pain in the end.

Join me as I attempt to climb out of the metaphorical hole that is my grief. The climb out of that metaphorical hole involves spiritual reflections and the comfort found in religious texts. We will share a candid discussion on the existential questions: Can I go on living? Do I have a choice?

I will present a poem, entitled "Blind," that I wrote in 1979, and how it amplifies the book's explorations of survival, regret, and hunger for meaning. Also, you will accompany me as I honestly confront myself regarding actions taken or not taken in her final days and reflection on moments when private discussions about her condition may have been overheard. Finally, together we will discover the catalyst for my redemption.

Chapter 1:
INTRODUCTION TO DEATH

In 1958 I was riding in the car with my brothers, Mom, and Dad. The car was a 1953 Studebaker. The dashboard was cluttered with many instruments I did not understand. It was finished in painted metal and trimmed in faux woodgrain. Integrated into the dashboard was a spacious glove box. It was so deep that whenever my mom would open it I would peer in expecting to see some creature lurking in the deep or to hear the echo of a coyote howling. The seating arrangement was such that Dad drove, Mom sat in the middle, and I sat in the front seat next to the passenger door. My brothers Delvin and Nelson were in the back seat. On this particular occasion I can't remember where we were going. However, Dad had to stop by one of his friends' houses so he pulled into the curb and parked. He got out of the car and went into the house. I sat there staring into the dash when suddenly the glove box door turned into what appeared to be a TV screen. There was a group of people assembled at a church. They were all wearing black and suddenly the minister spoke the words from John 11:25-26 (KJV), ". . . *I am the resurrection, and the life: he that believeth in me, though he were dead, yet shall he live: And whosoever liveth and believeth in me shall never die.*" The minister's voice was compelling, like the sonic boom that occurs after a jet passes over. Yet his voice was melodious. One could discern a deliberate cadence. He continued speaking these words from 1 Timothy 6:7 (KJV) "For we brought nothing into *this* world, *and it is* certain we can carry nothing out." The minister said these words as he preceded a pine box into the church and, reaching the pulpit, he stepped up into the pulpit and those carrying the pine box placed it on a table in front of the rostrum.

I found it eerily disconcerting that during the service depicted in this vision I could see no faces, and I can only remember the preacher's dress. He wore a black suit, with a black minister's shirt with a white tab on the collar. As people adjourned to the cemetery he put on a black minister's hat. In those days you could tell a minister when you saw him because he wore what I call the traditional uniform of a minister for those days.

All black with a minister's collar shirt. Also, his uniform would not be complete without the black hat that most ministers wore.

The scene at the cemetery was such that everyone stood around the grave. The minister stood at the head of the grave reciting these words from Genesis 3:9 (KJV):

> *In the sweat of thy face shalt thou eat bread, till thou return unto the ground; for out of it wast thou taken for dust thou art, and unto dust shalt thou return.*

The words seemed to echo in the cemetery, the minister's voice commanding attention. His authority was evident in his deportment and in his voice. One would think that God himself was speaking as he sprinkled the sand on the pine box. I could hear every grain of sand resound as it landed upon the pine box. I remember such a chilling feeling coming over me as the vision ended. I sat there, in the car with my mother and my brothers, in disbelief at what had just happened before my very eyes. I did not say a word. I didn't tell my mother or my brothers. I didn't tell anyone. I just sat there at that tender age having just witnessed what death is. Not from someone dying in my family but because God had chosen to reveal death to me in that manner in at that time. I didn't know what the vision meant. I didn't know at that time that I would one day be a minister, but I knew that I would never forget the vision that taught me about death and the funeral ceremony. Since that time, I have had to face the death of many loved ones, including my grandmother's death, my mother-in-law's death, my sister's, our daughter's death, and our niece's and my mother's death—but none of those deaths prepared me for what I feel now having lost Diane, my wife of 48 years.

When my grandmother died in 1964, I was only eleven years old. Grief was a stranger to me then, abstract and shapeless, hovering somewhere between confusion and numbness. Her passing felt sudden, a ripple that reached me before I even understood its source.

My first encounter with my paternal grandmother was itself a lesson in uncertainty. We had just returned from Spain, taking shelter on my maternal grandfather's plantation while we awaited my father's arrival aboard the USS Forrestal, soon to dock in Charleston, South Carolina.

One afternoon, as I played among the rows of corn and the sun cast shadows across the fields, a large black Cadillac rolled up the drive, its size and shine out of place on the dusty path. My mother introduced me to the woman who would become a recurring figure in my childhood summers. To my surprise, she explained that I would be spending the night with this lady, a breach of the family routine that usually kept us close to home. I remember climbing into the passenger seat, the unfamiliar scent of the car, the sensation of the plush upholstery beneath my hands. She spoke softly, telling me that her son was my father, and that, recognizing his absence in my life, she would try to fill the space he left behind. Looking back, I realize now how little I understood in that moment, sitting quietly beside her as we drove pass the Lily Tulip Company, the oversized cup at its entrance impossible to miss even for a child lost in thought. That first visit blurred into many others, a ritual that became the rhythm of my summers. In Augusta, she made the world gentle for me. She bought my school clothes and shoes, sometimes a toy, and always brought home treats, vanilla wafers, strawberries, and vanilla ice cream. Sundays meant church and the small, sacred comfort of my hand in hers.

The last summer I came to visit my grandmother, I realize now, she tried to tell me that she was dying. At the time, I noticed she seemed uncharacteristically withdrawn, her mood shadowed by a sadness I couldn't place. Once or twice, she snapped at me, a small, sharp break in her usual gentle manner that startled us both. Then, in an unguarded moment, tears welled up in her eyes and, with trembling words, she told me that when I returned the next summer, she would not be there. She spoke of leaving her house to me, and her car too, pressing these legacies into my young hands. At thirteen, the meaning slipped past me; her words were like a puzzle missing half of its pieces. She didn't make it to the next summer. In February, the news arrived: my grandmother was dead. Despite her meager resources my mother found a way for the two of us to travel to Augusta for the funeral. I remember the church surrounded by mourners, so many that we could scarcely approach the door. My mother pleaded with the crowd, explaining that the deceased's grandchild was here, and slowly, they parted to let me through. Inside, the pews were full, but a man, a deacon as I would later learn, took my hand kindly and led me to the section where the deacons sat. I remember sitting there, small and bewildered, the hum of voices and the shuffling of feet swirling around me. The service unfolded at a distance: I barely heard the minister's words, lost in the tremors of loss and the strangeness of my own presence among so many adults. Occasionally, my gaze drifted to the front pew, where my father and his wife sat, their faces carved with grief. In that crowded church, the reality of death began to take shape, a lesson not in words, but in the silent currents of sorrow and love that passed through generations. My grandmother's death left a quiet ache, a void that deepened as years passed and I faced loss again.

As the years wore on and I grew into adulthood, I came to learn a hard truth: the house and car my grandmother had spoken of never came to me. My grandfather confided in me, years later, that after she fell ill, my father and his wife had persuaded her to change her will while she was in the hospital. Yet even as I absorbed this, I found no bitterness in my heart. I never sought to profit from her passing; the thought of benefiting from her death felt hollow and wrong. For me, the true treasures she left behind were not measured in deeds or possessions, but in the gentle memories of vanilla wafers, summer afternoons, and the warmth of my hand in her hand at church. I have never valued material things above human life, and her memory remains far more precious than any inheritance could ever be.

August 22nd of 1988, I graduated from Augusta College with a major in sociology and a minor in social work. Diane and I decided to move to New York, where her mother lived and worked for the Transit Authority in Manhattan. We packed up the car with the two kids, Astra and Amber, and made the long drive north, our hearts full of hope for a new chapter. In those first weeks, we stayed with Diane's mother at 615 W 144th St. The apartment bustled with city sounds and the comforting rhythm of family life. Before long, I found work with the United Church of Christ on Madison Ave, and we secured our own place just up the street from my mother-in-law's apartment at 618 W 144th St. Life had a sense of possibility; the children were thriving, and Diane's mother's presence anchored our days.

Then, one afternoon as I sat at my desk, Diane called to say her mother needed to see a doctor. I knew she hadn't been feeling well and encouraged Diane to take her. Hours later, the phone rang again; this time, her voice trembled with something I could feel before she spoke. "Baby, Mama died." The words landed with a weight I wasn't prepared to carry. Diane described how, while leaving the doctor's office, her mother had collapsed at the bottom of some stairs. The medical staff rushed to aid her, but it was too late. The doctor said she was gone before she hit the floor.

I asked Diane where she was, got the address, and rushed to gather her, Astra and Amber. At the scene, disbelief had etched itself into Diane's face, her body shaking with grief and shock. I tried to steady her as we hailed a cab and returned home, both of us uncertain about what the future would hold and what steps we should take next.

We received a telephone call and were told that we needed to come down to the morgue and identify her mother's remains. I'll never forget that day one of her cousins and his wife drove us to the morgue. Diane and I had decided that I would go in and identify her mother's remains. I was a little taken back when her cousin, who was older, did not volunteer to go in with me. However, I showed no sign of foreboding as I exited the car and entered the doors into the morgue where a large sign greeted me that said, "Here Is Where the Living Learn from the Dead!" As I stood there mesmerized by those words my trance was broken when an attendant touched my shoulder and ushered me into a room with a glass window and a white curtain. The curtain was pulled back. A stretcher was rolled into the room and just for a moment the sheet covering the body on the stretcher was pulled back and her face uncovered so that I could identify the remains. I nodded my head to confirm her identity. I was waved off and I left the room, and then the building. I entered the car in silence as Diane took my hand, and I remained silent on the drive home.

In the silence that follows the events that transpire after a death, the initial shock gave way to long evenings filled with quiet grief, a simple but profound truth settled between us: Diane was all I had, and I was all she had. With her mother's sudden absence, the world seemed newly precarious, pared down to what was most essential. We leaned into each other, not just out of necessity, but out of a deep recognition that our survival, emotional and otherwise, depended on holding each other up.

My sister's death in 1984 had marked another turning point, a sorrow that still echoes quietly through the years. We had always been close, closer, perhaps, than siblings often are. I had made it my duty to shield her from the roughness of our brothers to step in between when tears threatened to fall. Even as adults, a protective tenderness lingered.

She had come home to Augusta, her two children in tow, escaping for a time the routines of Army life in Newport News, Virginia, where her husband was stationed. My sister had battled lupus for five years by then, weathering its unpredictability with a quiet resilience. Flare-ups would come, swollen feet and aching joints, but she managed, refusing to let illness define the landscape of her days.

I remember the afternoon she told me she was returning to Virginia. I was working as a taxi driver, waiting in my cab near the PX on Fort Gordon, when she pulled up beside me. "Elliott, I'm going back to Virginia," she said, and my concern was immediately validated, her feet were still swollen, and the thought of her navigating a five-speed car across state lines filled me with worry. She brushed it off with gentle confidence. "I'll be fine. Everything will be OK." I relented, though an uneasiness lingered in my chest. Before she left, she paused. "Wait a minute. Give me a hug." I did one last embrace, neither of us knowing it was goodbye. A short while after returning to Virginia a flare-up came. Her medical records say the wrong medication was given. Her lungs filled with fluid, and she suffocated. The finality of it all stunned me, and left me wishing I had held her a moment longer.

Her loss taught me the necessity of open affection, the necessity of showing people how much they are loved. The regret of words left unsaid, hugs left ungiven, is a quiet ache that never fully leaves. These lessons, hard-earned and etched in the fabric of loss, remind me again and again to treasure the warmth of being in the presence of our loved ones and that we should express that love daily.

Our daughter Astra's death was a sorrow distinct from all others, a pain that seemed to ripple backward and forward through time, reshaping every memory and every hope. Astra had always been determined, resilient; she'd just returned from ROTC training at Quantico, Virginia, moving through the house with her usual sense of purpose. Yet, within days, the brightness in her dimmed. Tiredness overtook her, her energy flagging, her joints aching in inexplicable ways. We thought perhaps she had overtrained or caught a virus while away. The doctor agreed. The doctor prescribed medication and told us to let her rest. For a brief spell, there was hope: her symptoms eased, and we let ourselves believe it was only a passing illness. But two days later her knees locked, her legs weakened, and she could hardly walk. The fear that had lingered at the edges of our minds now took root. We went back to the doctor, and this time, lab work was ordered. I'll never forget the way the doctor regarded us when we returned for the results of the lab work his face displayed a canvas of concern. "Astra has tested positive for lupus," he said gently. The words struck with a chilling familiarity; my sister, too, had battled and lost to this relentless disease. We were referred to the Medical College of Georgia's rheumatology specialists, who placed Astra on medication and sent her home with guarded instructions. She was diagnosed in February. On March 4th, she died.

Those days and nights spent nursing her through flare-ups, watching over her as she drifted between pain and restless sleep, were a crucible. In the long hours, I became deeply aware of a presence, a Comforter, that seemed to arrive just when despair threatened to overtake me. "The Lord is my shepherd; I shall not want." Those words threaded through my mind and my prayers, a lifeline in the darkness.

Grief after Astra's passing was not quiet; it thundered and echoed, a grief made sharper by the cruel repetition of fate. But even as loss hollowed out our world, I clung to the faith that had sustained me through previous storms, the knowledge that even in the deepest valleys we are not bereft of comfort. The ache of her absence, the memory of her courage, and the presence of those steadfast words became my shelter as the days blurred past.

Diane, my steadfast anchor: A willing hand of compassion in an otherwise void existence. In the midst of unspeakable loss, when each day felt hollowed out by grief, she was my shelter, a quiet presence that kept me tethered to what little remained of hope. Her gentleness did not erase pain, but it shaped it into something bearable, a sorrow softened by the warmth of understanding and companionship. Even as waves of heartache threatened to sweep me away, Diane's constancy allowed me to stay afloat; her hands, always ready to steady mine, reminded me that love persists even in the starkest seasons of absence.

Aimee was my sister Giovanna's daughter, the first-born among all the children, a child who in many ways felt like our own first baby. When she arrived, we surrounded Giovanna with love and support, helping care for tiny Aimee as she grew into a spirited young girl. After my sister's passing from lupus, our family gathered around Aimee even more closely, helping my mother raise her. She found her footing, thriving with a quiet determination that echoed her mother's resilience. Aimee graduated from high school and inspired by her grandfather's example, entered the United States Navy as a Petty Officer storekeeper, taking great pride in her service.

Her years in the Navy were marked by the same resolve, even as she began to face a gauntlet of medical issues: endometriosis, persistent pain, and what her doctors believed was a connective tissue disorder. For years, she underwent treatment, her diagnosis shifting and evolving, until finally, after her health severely limited her ability to serve, she was medically diagnosed with lupus and released from active duty. Yet, she did not let that define her. For five years afterward, Aimee continued to hope for a return to service, traveling regularly to the Norfolk Naval Hospital for evaluations. Each visit carried the possibility of a new direction, a sliver of hope that the Navy might yet call her back. But in 2010, the decision was made final: Aimee was medically retired, both from the Navy and from the United States Postal Service. She lived in Winston-Salem, North Carolina, where she sought care from civilian doctors, adapting as best she could to a new rhythm of life. She remained diligent, driving to appointments, advocating for her health, and refusing to let lupus eclipse her identity. Yet, we watched with growing concern as her condition worsened, the disease's reach creeping further and further into the fabric of her body. Aimee finally relocated to Augusta to be with us, but lupus had already spread to her brain. The move came too late; not long after her arrival, she was hospitalized, and then, heartbreakingly, she was gone. In the aftermath, I remember the doctor's earnest plea, urging me to tell any family member with lupus to seek care in a place equipped to handle such a relentless disease. The doctor exclaimed, "If you had gotten Aimee here sooner," she said, "she might have had a chance." That conversation remains etched in my memory, a reminder of both the cruel limitations of circumstance and the vital necessity of specialized care. Aimee 's life was marked not only by struggle and loss, but by courage, perseverance, and the steadfast bonds of family that carried her through. Her story, like those of my sister and daughter, weaves another thread of love and loss into the fabric of our lives, teaching us, over and over again, the preciousness of time, the importance of vigilance, and the enduring strength we find in one another.

October 29th, 2019, my mother died, and with her passing, language itself seemed to abandon me. There were no words vast enough to contain the ache, no phrases sturdy enough to shoulder all that sudden silence. But in those final months, as Sundowner's disease wove confusion into her days, she managed—clear and resolute—to gift me a promise: "I promise you that I will do the best that I can to take care of myself for as long as I can." Her voice, even then, was the same voice that had carried me through every season of my life—unbowed by hardship, fiercely independent, quietly loving.

In the beginning, it was just me and Mom. She was not married when I was born, so she became my entire world, my teacher, my anchor, my guide. At four or five, she sat me down with the serious gravity of someone entrusting a secret, and told me that one day, she would not be with me. She wanted me to know how to survive, how to stand on my own. She taught me to cook, to iron my shirts, to scrub the floor until it shone. Her lessons were woven into the fabric of daily living, each skill a thread of self-reliance. I remember the sting of a spanking once, a punishment for not mastering long division, a task she herself could not do. The irony of it was not lost on me, even then, but the lesson endured: always try your best, and never shy from effort, no matter how daunting. Though she married eventually, she insisted I remain independent, never to rely on anyone, never to portray a hint of weakness. She didn't chastise me if I cried, but she let me know I should not let the world see me falter. That same strength she instilled in me became my armor, the thing that steadied my hands as I made her final arrangements, saw to every detail with the same resolve she had demanded of me. It was her legacy: a strength that did not preclude tenderness, a resolve that made space for sorrow but refused to let it define me.

What I learned from my mother's death, from the echo of her words, "I promise I am going to do the best that I can for myself as long as I can," was that independence is not isolation; it is devotion to oneself and to those we love. She remained true to this until her final days, only allowing me to intervene when she could no longer carry the burden alone. All that I am, all the strength I muster, I owe to her. She taught me how to be resilient, how to navigate the world without apology. Through her, I learned that even in the face of loss, love endures, and the lessons of those who raise us shape the very core of who we become.

Chapter 2:
THE DAY EVERYTHING CHANGED

In August 2024 my wife's health took an unexpected turn. What began as a mild discomfort escalated into a debilitating illness within weeks. She grew increasingly weak, unable to stand or walk without assistance. Concerned, I took her to our primary care doctor. After arriving at the doctor's office, we waited in the waiting room with several other patients. The waiting room was large, with big glass windows that bathed the space in warm sunlight, momentarily easing the tension that hung thick in the air. Soon, a nursing assistant called us back. She gently asked my wife to step onto the scale, her voice calm and steady, a small kindness in the midst of uncertainty. After recording her weight, the assistant led us to a treatment room, where she took my wife's height, blood pressure, pulse, and respirations. Her motions were practiced and efficient.

She asked my wife several questions about her pain: How severe was it? Where exactly did it hurt? Had her medications changed at all? My wife answered as best she could, her responses measured but tinged with fatigue. The assistant listened, noting each detail, and completed her preliminary examination with a reassuring word. Once she finished, she guided us to another room to wait for the doctor: another pause, another hush before the next wave of news. The doctor, after a thorough examination, referred us to a gastroenterologist.

The referral felt both urgent and unsettling, underscoring the gravity of her symptoms and the uncertainty looming ahead. The day we arrived at the gastroenterologist's office; my wife was relying on a rollator to move. Although the doctor wasn't available, we were fortunate to be seen by his physician's assistant (PA). The PA, alarmed by my wife's condition, summoned the doctor immediately. His advice was firm and urgent: take her straight to the emergency room.

The emergency room was a chaotic scene of coughing patients, bustling reception staff, and janitors maintaining cleanliness. As we waited for our turn, I observed people seeking absence excuses for work, their concerns trivial compared to the gravity of our situation.

Once admitted, the initial diagnosis was dehydration, a seemingly simple issue. After 24 hours in the emergency room, Diane insisted that I go home to shower and change clothes. While I was gone, a series of lab results revealed the devastating truth: my wife's white blood cell count was critically low, and there were several spots on her lungs and one on her liver. The diagnosis was metastatic cancer. What concerned me most was leaving my wife alone in such a vulnerable state, even for a brief time to shower and change clothes at home.

I had made it clear to the hospital staff before I left: I wanted to be present when the results, the CT scan, lab work, and any diagnoses, were shared with my wife. Yet my request was ignored. During my absence, one of the emergency room doctors entered her room alone, without a social worker, nurse, or even the smallest gesture of compassion. Lacking any comforting bedside manner, the doctor abruptly delivered the devastating news: my wife had metastatic cancer. The shock and pain she must have felt on hearing this, without a loved one by her side, haunts me still. It was as if a bomb had been dropped, the full weight of the diagnosis landing on her shoulders with no support to soften the blow. She called me on the telephone expressing her shock and pain at how callous the doctor was.

Naturally I rushed back to her side, my mind racing with worry and anger, desperate to offer whatever comfort I could. I found her sitting in silence, her eyes searching my face for reassurance, her hands trembling with the weight of the news. I tried to be a steady presence, holding her hand and listening as she recounted every word, every gesture, that had compounded her distress in those lonely moments. We sat together in that stark hospital room, the world narrowing to the space between us as we processed the diagnosis and the way it had been delivered. There was no right way to react, no script for grief this sudden and raw. But in that moment, I knew that what mattered most was being present for her, offering the warmth and connection so absent in the doctor's approach.

Eventually, we gathered our resolve and began to consider the road ahead. Thankfully, our children were by our sides. They took a lot of the weight off our shoulders by notifying family and putting appointments on our calendars. I do not know how we would have managed without them. In those first bewildering days, their presence formed a protective circle around us, buffering us from the practical chaos, the barrage of messages, the flood of decisions, the endless coordination that accompanies a diagnosis so grave. With their help, we could focus on supporting each other, gathering whatever strength we had left for the journey ahead.

The days that followed were filled with treatment plans being outlined, anxious conversations, medical briefings, and the slow, deliberate assembling of hope in the face of uncertainty. The oncologist confirmed that the cancer was treatable. She explained that all metastatic cancer is considered stage four, emphasizing both the seriousness and urgency of the diagnosis. Although the cancer was fast-growing, she reassured us that it often responds well to the right therapies. Without delay, she outlined an aggressive treatment protocol and assured us that they would begin immediately, offering a glimmer of hope amid the uncertainty.

Together, my wife and I resolved to fight. Though we found ourselves in a different doctor's office, the atmosphere felt eerily familiar. Just four years earlier, we had sat in another sterile room as a doctor delivered the news that I had multiple myeloma. Without hesitation, my wife turned to me and declared, "We're going to fight." She then looked at the doctor and firmly repeated, "That's our decision, we're going to fight." Now, here we were again, facing the same relentless adversary. Yet our determination remained unchanged: we would fight. It was uncanny how history seemed to be repeating itself, but in the face of this new challenge, our resolve was as steadfast as ever.

The very first day of treatment required seven and a half hours in the infusion room. The next three days, she spent decreasing amounts of time receiving treatments, culminating in weekly lab visits for an injection. Her treatments began with a rigorous infusion regimen involving steroids, targeted cancer medications, and fluids administered to guard against dehydration.

Each visit to the infusion center felt like stepping into a labyrinth of protocols and precautions. The nurses would review a checklist of medications, one to counter inflammation, another to attack rapidly dividing cells, yet another to shield her stomach from harsh side effects. It seemed as if every remedy demanded its own attendant protector: a drug to make sure her body tolerated the cancer therapy, another to stave off the nausea or fever that might otherwise accompany the powerful infusions.

Among all the side effects, one of the most relentless was the severe constipation brought on by her medications. We tried every approach, probiotics, laxatives, carefully adjusted diets, seeking any solution that would bring lasting relief, but each remedy seemed to offer only a fleeting respite. Some would work for a few days, providing a glimmer of hope, only to lose their effect, leaving us right back where we started. It became clear that constipation was not just a discomfort, but a stubborn adversary of its own, one that overshadowed every other challenge she faced. Still, we were undeterred, determined to keep searching for answers and ways to ease her burden, even as this most persistent of symptoms tested our patience and resolve.

Navigating this intricate regimen became our new normal. I watched as she bravely endured each cycle, her spirit unyielding even when her body grew weary. The strength it took just to weather a single treatment was humbling, and yet she faced every round determined, sometimes quietly, sometimes with flashes of humor that cut through the clinical monotony. We learned to track side effects, monitor her temperature, adjust her diet, and to keep a log of symptoms for the doctors. There were days when the medications left her exhausted, but there were also mornings when we glimpsed a return of her old vitality, brief respites that fueled our hope.

Instructions and warnings came in a steady stream, their complexity a testament to both the potency of modern medicine and its limitations. We were amazed at how swift her recovery was. By mid-October, she had regained her strength to the point where she could move about independently. The pain in her side had subsided, and the inflammation in her liver had diminished as well.

As life resumed, we returned to cherished traditions, such as preparing our holiday feast together, a ritual we thought impossible just weeks earlier. But first things first. We needed to get the Christmas decorations up. Each year, decking the house in festive cheer was more than just a tradition, it was a declaration of hope, a way to claim a little light even in the darkest season. We love to get our Christmas decorations up early. That way we could enjoy them longer before taking them down. That year the gentle glow of twinkling lights and the scent of pine seemed to hold special significance. Moving deliberately, we unpacked ornaments collected over decades, each one a memory, a testament to resilience and joy.

The process itself was healing, a pause between doctor's appointments and medication schedules, a chance to create something beautiful together. No wonder we were married on December 25th, 1976! Christmas was our favorite time of year. Over the decades, that season became a tapestry of tradition and togetherness, an anchor through every storm and celebration. Each holiday seemed to gather all the threads of our lives, weaving laughter and comfort into the coldest days.

Our holiday cooking began in earnest. Together, we prepared hash, a savory blend of pork, beef, chicken, onions, ketchup, and potatoes. Each ingredient was measured with care, five pounds apiece, and seasoned with our secret mix of spices. As we cooked, old memories resurfaced. I learned the art of making hash in my childhood, assisting my great-grandfather during those long nights of cooking a whole hog on an open pit. I can still recall those evenings vividly: after my great-grandfather and the others had finished preparing the hog for the pit, tasks I was too small to help with, they would settle in, content and drowsy from homemade moonshine. By midnight, it always seemed I was the only one awake and alert enough to tend the hog, mopping it with vinegar and pepper, rousing the others as needed to help turn the hog so it wouldn't burn. Those quiet, smoky hours were when I first learned the secret to making hash, back when it simmered in a heavy black cauldron, like the ones witches use in old television shows. Those traditions, passed down through generations, became the cornerstone of our own celebrations, flavoring each holiday with the heritage and memory.

By October, we focused on preparing collard greens cooked with smoked ham hocks. We would clean the collards with a little bit of dish-washing detergent. We made sure to rinse them thoroughly. Two cups of chicken broth would be brought to a boil in a Dutch oven. The ham hocks which had been baked in the oven would simmer in the chicken broth until they fell apart. The collards would slowly be added to the broth and ham hocks so that the first collards to be introduced to the mixture would cook down before any more were added.

We prepared the turnip greens next with smoked turkey wings. The turkey wings were allowed to cook apart in chicken broth. We did not use as much broth as we use for collards because the turnips seem to produce more natural water. We always made sure that we cooked foods that everyone could eat. The greens, frozen in advance, were staples of our family celebrations. Some people do not eat pork so collards cooked with ham hocks would not be acceptable to that person. We love to cook because we love to eat. The cook is always the best person fed.

Next came my wife's special Macaroni and Cheese. It is a meticulous process involving layers of perfectly seasoned al-dente macaroni, butter, sour cream, and a roux enriched with sharp and extra sharp cheeses. The process begins with me slicing cheese the day before. We use five or six pounds of cheese and as you can imagine trying to slice it all, to say a quarter of an inch thick evenly is quite a chore with a butcher's knife. But somehow, I managed to get it done. I would take breaks in between each pound. I'd stand up for a part of the time which allowed me to get more leverage on the knife. And then sit down for the other part of the time. I got it done. We also keep the different types of cheese separated so that when we layer the Macaroni and Cheese we put even amounts of sharp and extra sharp cheese into each one. We would start by placing a layer of macaroni in the bottom of a pan then layering it with the regular cheese then another layer of macaroni layer with the extra sharp cheese another layer of macaroni layered with sharp cheese and finally a layer of Macaroni and topping it all with a layer of extra sharp cheese covering the entire pan. The Macaroni and Cheese would be extra cheesy because we would bathe it in sour cream before we start layering it into the pan. Finally, we pour the roux down into the pan. Not too much, because you don't want it to boil over in the oven. But about halfway up the pan so that as it cooks all of the macaroni is bathed in the roux. A couple of things that my wife always reminded me of is that when we boil the water for macaroni make sure to place enough oil in it so that the macaroni doesn't stick together. Second, make sure that there is enough salt in the water. You never get a second chance to season pasta. She would say one of the keys to it is that you're going to pour the water off and most of the salt is going to be in the water. So, you got to make sure that the macaroni is seasoned adequately. Finally, she would say you don't want your macaroni mushy. So, to ensure it is al-dente, take your fork and press the macaroni against the side of your pot after 5 minutes if it breaks smoothly and with just enough pressure that's al-dente. You don't want it to get to the point where you mash the macaroni against the side of the pot, and it looks like mashed potatoes.

December 2024 marked our 48th anniversary, a joyous occasion celebrated amidst good food and the warmth and love of family.

January arrived with hope. We had planned to go to Hilton Head Island to celebrate our anniversary. December 25th is our anniversary, but we like to celebrate Christmas and New Years at home and leave January 2nd to go and celebrate our anniversary. However, Lady Di was not feeling up to the trip, so we stayed home. By mid-month, my wife's health began to decline again. Her doctor decided that because she had responded so well to the treatment before, she would put her on maintenance medication. Immediately after the first maintenance infusion my wife got sicker. It was as if she was allergic to the maintenance medication. Her doctor decided to stop the maintenance medication and try a new regimen. But the damage had already been done. Her liver swelled, causing discomfort that made lying in bed unbearable. She spent her days in her recliner, battling pain that grew increasingly severe. It soon got to the point where she could not lie in bed at all. Her days and nights were spent in the recliner. Tylenol offered temporary relief, but stronger medications became necessary, first codeine-based mixtures, then pure morphine.

The morphine dulled her pain but left her drowsy, weak, and disoriented. Fearing to leave her alone, I enlisted the help of my daughters when I had appointments or when I went to preach on Sundays. Despite these measures, her condition worsened. By February, the cancer spread further affecting her liver, lungs, and even her fourth vertebra.

It was during this time that I remembered that one morning as I was performing my morning devotional. I heard a voice singing. The voice sing: "*Walk with me Lord, walk with me, while I'm on this tedious journey I want Jesus to walk with me.*" There was a refrain that said, "*Walk with me Lord, walk with me. Walk with me Lord, walk with me while I'm on this pilgrim's journey. I want Jesus to walk with me.*" I was startled because there was no one in the room but me. I looked around the room anxiously searching for the source of the singing. I knew it could not be me because I can't sing! Also, the lyrics of the song were not familiar to me. However, as reality set in it became apparent that I was singing a song that I don't remember ever hearing before. I questioned the origin of the song, asking myself who is that singing? And then answering myself by saying "Shush, fool: that's the Holy Ghost." After I finished singing the song I picked up my cell phone and Googled the words "walk with me Lord" only to find to my surprise that there is a song called "Walk With Me, Lord." That song, like the scriptures that God put in my mind during tragedies, provided some measure of comfort doing this difficult time.

Her new treatment regimen included radiation for the vertebra, but the days leading to these appointments were marked by relentless pain. Her time was spent mostly in her recliner, the morphine unable to provide complete relief.

On March 11, 2025, her pain escalated to an unbearable level. At 2:00 AM, guided by divine inspiration, I shaved, showered, and called 911 to have her taken to the emergency room. I called an ambulance because I did not want to make her uncomfortable by wrestling her into the car.

In the emergency room her condition was dire. Numerous tests revealed the cancer had spread to her brain. At 7:00 AM, the doctor delivered the heartbreaking prognosis to my family: the cancer was terminal. I stayed by her side as she was moved to a hospital room, where the struggle continued. Her pain persisted despite medical interventions, and the morphine offered fleeting comfort. I was exhausted by this time. Our daughters had been with me constantly in the process. Our son arrived and we all conducted a vigil. And when it appeared that the morphine drip was giving her some relief, as we deduced by her quiet and stillness not crying out in pain, we decided to go home and get some rest as she slept.

On March 14, 2025, we received the call that shattered my world: my wife had passed away. In that moment, I felt an overwhelming sense of guilt for not being there when she took her final breath. I was reminded of Matthew 26:36-40 (KJV) where Jesus prays in Gethsemane:

> *"Then cometh Jesus with them unto a place called Gethsemane, and saith unto the disciples, sit ye here, while I go and pray yonder.*
>
> *And he took with him Peter and the two sons of Zebedee and began to be sorrowful and very heavy.*

*Then saith he unto them, my soul is exceeding sorrowful,
even unto death: tarry ye here, and watch with me.*

*And he went a little further, and fell on his face, and
prayed, saying, O my Father, if it be possible, let this cup
pass from me: nevertheless, not as I will, but as thou wilt.*

*And he cometh unto the disciples, and findeth them asleep,
and saith unto Peter, what, could ye not watch with me
one hour?"*

Like Peter I had gotten tired and grown weak. I had failed. A simple thing that I know she would have done for me, I had not been able to do for her. Stay awake. Sometimes we rush as we read scriptures. We don't take the time to realize how profound the emotions and the content of the scripture are. For example, Jesus says, *my soul is exceeding sorrowful, even unto death. Wait here and watch with Me.* He was asking Peter and the others to help him by sharing this burden. But they were tired and fell asleep. In that instance Jesus was all alone left to bear the pain of the knowledge of the coming crucifixion and separation from God alone. Jesus's words, *"What, could ye not watch with me one hour?"* are an indication of hurt or disappointed he felt. Just as I understand the hurt and disappointment of Jesus in this instance, I felt that I had disappointed my wife at a time when she needed me.

The emptiness left by her passing is unlike anything I have ever known. On the numerous occasions that I had faced death in the past; she had been there with me. She would hold my hand and allow me to lean my head on her shoulder. Now I was alone. What could I do? How could I stand through this tragedy? Can I go on? Do I want to go on? Do I have a choice? The love we shared for 48 years shaped my existence. She had always been just a telephone call away. When I didn't know what to do, I could call her. When I saw something that I thought might amuse her I could call her. When I felt something that I didn't quite understand I could call her. Now, what would I do?

The gulf created by her death and her absence feels irreplaceable. Since her death grief has been my unwavering companion. It walks with me through every day, a constant echo of the love and life we shared. People often ask if things have "returned to normal," but how can they?

She was (and remains) irreplaceable. There is no pathway back to life that is untouched by her absence, no normal to reclaim when the very foundation of my world shifted so profoundly. Normalcy, as it was when she was with me, is an impossibility. So, in response to their question about "normalcy" I can only offer silence. Yet, amidst the sorrow, I hold onto the memories of her strength, resilience, and love, qualities that will forever inspire and guide me.

The routines of life that once seemed mundane now carried a weight that was unbearable. Tasks like scheduling pest control appointments, which had always been her domain, now fell solely to me, a reminder of her absence. The act of picking up the phone, flipping through the calendar, and settling on a date felt like a hollow echo of a shared partnership.

When the pest control technician arrived and offered his condolences, I found myself grappling with the surreal moment when he said he thought he had seen her sitting in the recliner, her usual spot. It was a fleeting, almost ghostly acknowledgment of her presence, or rather, the absence that filled the room like a shadow.

Every action, every decision, became a quiet confrontation with the question of how to keep moving forward. While the external world expected business as usual, my internal world had shifted irrevocably. The loneliness was profound, and the search for meaning amidst the grief was unrelenting. It was as though each passing day led me deeper into a void that I struggled to understand, a hole that seemed impossible to escape.

Every once in a while, I would hear that voice singing, *"Walk with me Lord, walk with me, while I'm on this tedious journey, I won't Jesus to walk with me."* And for a few fleeting moments I received a reprieve from the grief allowing me to carry on with the mundane duties of everyday life. I thank God for His gift of the Holy Spirit.

The weight of survival often carries burdens far beyond the physical. I remember the day I received my diagnosis of multiple myeloma. It was the kind of news that shifts the axis of your world, that makes time stand still. In 2020, I found hope in the sterile halls of the Veterans Hospital in Nashville, Tennessee, where I underwent a stem cell transplant. I knew the risks; I knew that 3% of patients undergoing this procedure would not make it. But I lived. That thought, the mere fact of surviving, became a double-edged sword as I faced the tragedy of losing my wife years later.

The questions began to haunt me. Why was I spared while she was taken? Could it be that somehow, she had traded her life for mine? This notion, as irrational as it seemed, rooted itself deep in my mind. Her unwavering selflessness in our conversations took on a haunting significance. Every time I asked her if she was okay, she would deflect the question, asking instead, "Are you okay?" When I assured her, I was, she simply replied, "That's all that matters."

Her words, though comforting at the time, now replay in my mind with a haunting clarity. It was only later that she began answering my questions honestly, yet she never failed to circle back to my wellbeing, as if her own struggles were secondary to mine. Did she know something I didn't? Was she silently bearing the weight of her illness, choosing instead to focus on keeping me alive, keeping me steady?

The thought that she might have made some cosmic bargain, willingly taking my place, is one I cannot shake. Her quiet strength, her ability to prioritize my health even as hers waned, feels like more than mere devotion—it feels like sacrifice. Why her and not me? This question, unanswered and perhaps unanswerable, is one I carry as I navigate the grief of her absence and the strange, hollow victory of my own survival. I fear there is another question created by that dialog. The words "*my own survival.*" Is that an accurate statement? I know it remains to be seen if I can survive without her. It is a presupposition to say "*my own survival*" because at this point that statement is questionable. I constantly assure myself that I am OK however only time will determine whether I actually survive or not.

Chapter 3:
THE HOLE THAT SWALLOWS

Grief carves out a place in the soul, a metaphorical hole where despair gathers like an endless abyss. For me, it wasn't just the loss of my wife that plunged me into this chasm; it was the haunting silence that followed, and the growing void that consumed every sense of normalcy in life. This hole revealed itself not only in moments of solitude but also in unexpected experiences, like the long, engrossing hours spent reading. Immersed in a narrative, I felt as though I slipped further into the depths of that hole, disconnected from the world around me. Emerging from the pages, I would find myself still trapped in isolation, as if the act of rejoining society required an agonizing climb out of the darkness. That agonizing climb out of the darkness reconnected me with the world slowly. It was like getting into a swimming pool. First you put your big toe in the water. Then the rest of your toes and then maybe both feet It is a meticulous process that could take seconds or minutes depending on whether you decide to just take the plunge. Conversations felt foreign. I understood what people were saying. However, it seemed as if I had no emotion to share. Participating in the flow of everyday life seemed as distant and unreachable as the sunlight filtering through the top of the hole.

The hole was an uninvited companion, an echo chamber for every thought of guilt and disbelief. I struggled to forgive myself for being alive, for carrying on while she could not. It was an inner turmoil that refused to relent, whispering questions I could not answer: "Why her and not me? How can I move forward when this pain feels so permanent? Is survival even a victory when it's shadowed by loss?" The isolation was compounded by the surreal disbelief of her absence. Her voice, once a constant comfort, had been silenced by finality. I found myself repeating those harrowing words in numbing cycles: "My wife is dead. My wife is dead."

The Wednesday night before she died carried a special kind of agony. The memory of leaving her at the hospital for what would be the last time remains etched in my mind. Sitting in the driveway of our home, I was overwhelmed by the oppressive realization that life had shifted irrevocably. "Is this my new normal?" I wondered in disbelief. The house felt like a shell, an echoing emptiness that my son's arrival could not fill. Guilt surged through me with suffocating clarity, as I questioned everything, even the nature of love and commitment itself. "Why get married," I pondered bitterly, "if it only leads to this unbearable pain?"

Silence became its own language, a brutal reminder of her absence. It was in this silence that the hole expanded, swallowing emotions, hopes, and even the most basic sense of self. There were moments when I felt nothing at all, a vast emptiness stretching endlessly within me. To climb out of the hole required more than physical effort; it demanded a reckoning with the grief that seemed insurmountable. It demanded acceptance of a reality that still felt unreal, a reality where her laugh, her beauty, her presence, her voice, could no longer be reached.

Forgiveness, too, seemed to reside at the bottom of the hole, buried far beneath the layers of guilt and despair. How could I forgive myself for living when she could not? How could I reconcile the unfairness of her absence with the hollow victory of my survival? Each attempt to escape the abyss was met with the weight of these questions that neither time nor logic could answer. The hole wasn't just about grief; it became a metaphor for the struggle to find meaning in a world that felt devoid of it. It symbolized the isolation that grief imposes, the separation from a former self and from society. It was a place where silence roared and loneliness stretched endlessly, where normal conversations and daily engagements felt like distant dreams. In this darkness, climbing out of the hole required more than a return to routine; it required a renewal of purpose, a way to coexist with the grief rather than be consumed by it. Though the ascent was slow and the summit often obscured, each step upward was an act of defiance against the void, a declaration of life amidst loss. But even now, the hole remains a part of me a reminder of love, sacrifice, and the enduring weight of grief.

Amid this metaphorical hole, where despair felt infinite and each step upward seemed futile, a fragment of scripture began to resonate within me. The words of Job, spoken in the face of unspeakable loss, *"Naked I came from my mother's womb, and naked I shall return. Blessed be the name of the Lord,"* echoed like a distant yet steady voice through the darkness. At first I struggled to grasp their meaning, burdened as I was by questions of fairness and the silent accusations of my grief. But as I repeated them, their cadence became a lifeline, a quiet balm to my fractured soul. The words reminded me that I had come into this world with nothing, I had a life that was borrowed, a life given to me--not something that I earned. Also, those words reminded me that death is inevitable. And somewhere in all of the thoughts invoked by those words, I realized that I deserve nothing that the fact that I had 48-plus wonderful years with a woman that God had given me when some people don't have any time at all. I had the privilege to experience the profound love that I experienced with Lady Di. In that instance I felt blessed and undeserving of the love that God had allowed me to receive from such a special lady. Comforting as the words where they did not erase the pain or fill the gaping void. However, the words of the scripture offer a new perspective, a humbling acknowledgment of life's impermanence and the mysterious balance of its blessings and losses. It was as though those words were a helping hand, extended not to pull me out in one swift motion, but to guide me gently upward, one painstaking inch at a time. They became my anchor, a reminder that even in profound despair, there remained a thread of continuity, a reason to keep climbing. The words did not produce a sudden transformation, nor were they accompanied by moments of instantaneous revelation. Rather, as the scripture soaked in there was the quiet comfort of those words repeating in my mind, softening the harsh edges of grief and helping me to coexist with the pain while finding the strength to face another day. That scripture became the first ripple in the still, stagnant pond of my sorrow. A pebble breaking the stillness of that stagnant pond hinting that perhaps the climb out of the hole, though arduous, was possible after all.

Chapter 4:
THE HEALING BREATH

As I navigated through the labyrinth of grief, another pattern began to emerge. A physical response to the emotional torrent. My body, in its intuitive wisdom, seemed to employ a safeguard against the strain of unrelenting sorrow. I noticed my breathing, subtle yet deliberate, shifting into what I later recognized as inspirational breaths. These breaths, drawn deeply and expelled slowly, offered a fleeting reprieve, an anchor amidst the chaos of invasive thoughts. Though involuntary, these breaths were deliberately drawn by my body.

Each time the memory of her solitary hospital room consumed me, her frail form cushioned by morphine, the doctor's solemn words echoing in my ears, I unconsciously leaned on these breaths and the scriptures that resounded in my head, "*Naked I came, naked I shall return blessed be the name of the Lord*" A breath, drawn deeply and expelled slowly. This combination punctuated the darkness, momentarily lifting the weight that bore down on my chest. I recalled my training as a combat medic, where we learned about the power of breathing to regulate stress in dire moments. Now, this physiological instinct became a lifeline, bridging the gap between despair and the faintest semblance of calm.

As I sat in our driveway one night, I had no recollection of the drive home. I do not remember what route I drove, if I obeyed traffic signals or the description of any cars I may have encountered before turning into our driveway. The driveway, once a testament to shared triumphs, now mirrored my internal landscape. Its emptiness became a reflection of my world, a world robbed of light, purpose, and direction. Even as porch lights glimmered from neighboring homes and passing cars whispered of life beyond my sorrow, I remained cocooned in darkness, both external and internal. The external darkness was represented by a numbness that did not allow me to experience any sensation. The internal darkness was represented by the macabre, a feeling of dread. It was as if all light had suddenly been drained from my world and all that was left was a dark curtain that could never be pulled back. It was as if my sense of sight, touch, taste, hearing, and smell had suddenly abandoned me. Yet, each breath seemed to push back the walls of this suffocating cavern, granting me a heartbeat's worth of clarity amidst the chaos. The breaths, mingled with the constant flow of scripture that I recited, provided by the Holy Spirit to soothe my fractured spirit and the lyric to the song "Walk With Me Lord," became a paradoxical union of physical and spiritual solace. They did not erase the guilt or silence the onslaught of memories, but they offered a rhythm, a cadence, that steadied me in the storm. And so, as the days and nights stretched on, I began to see how these breaths, this unconscious act of self-preservation, became my body's way of saying, "Keep climbing. Keep breathing. Keep living."

Chapter 5:
LOVE AND DOUBT

Love, in its purest form, has the power to define us, to shape us into beings capable of profound joy and profound sorrow. Diane was the embodiment of such love for me, she was a presence so deep and so consuming that it felt as though the very fabric of my soul had been stitched together with threads of her existence. From the moment our eyes met, I was transformed. Her gaze, dark and rich, held a universe so unfathomable that I could barely breathe under its weight. It was not merely her beauty that captivated me, though it was undeniable; it was the essence of her, the way her laughter seemed to mend the broken parts of my life, the way her gentle touch erased the sharp edges of pain. Her love defined me by changing me from the hard shell that I was and shaping me into a being who could express love for others. The threads of her existence sutured the lacerations deep in my soul thus piercing my hard shell. My life, broken as it was, was mended by her gentle touch. The words "I love you" now spring effortlessly from lips that once held them captive.

Our lives intertwined in ways that made the world feel both infinite and intimate. There was an unspoken language between us, a rhythm that only our hearts understood. She knew my thoughts before I could voice them, and I recognized her needs before she could articulate them. It was a bond so unique, so sacred, that even the simplest of gestures, a glass of water placed in her hands before she could ask for it. Her fingers gently squeezing mine in moments of distress, became declarations of devotion.

Yet love, as I have learned, is rarely simple. It is intricate, demanding, and often entwined with doubt. There were times, fleeting though they were, when I questioned my worthiness of her affection. Did I love her enough? Did she know, truly know, the depth of my feelings? The mind, in its vulnerability, is quick to plant seeds of uncertainty even amid the most fertile grounds of love. Even now, in her absence, my heart wrestles with these questions. But as I sit with the weight of her memory I am reminded of the truth, the way she called me her best friend to anyone who cared to listen. The way she sacrificed for me and the way she made me feel whole. It is through this lens, both painful and beautiful, that I begin to unravel the complexity of love and loss. She gave up everything for me. Her devotion can never be measured; her sacrifice can never be matched.

Love, profound as it was, became both my anchor and my tempest. It held me steady in moments of joy but churned within me during times of despair. Her love anchors me during times of doubt. When I am unsure if I can go on, I can hear her voice urging me onward. When she was serious her alto voice would permeate the walls of home as she said, "Boy you better go on and do what we said you were going to do!" Her love is the tempest that drives me when depression saps my energy. Her love allows me to keep climbing as if I am driven by the winds of a tempest. The love we shared, its depth and breadth, is unparalleled, yet it is also the source of my deepest doubts. I find myself caught in an endless loop of questions: Did she feel my love as deeply as I felt it for her? Did my actions convey the immensity of what I held in my heart, or were they mere shadows of what could have been?

Love, I've come to realize, is a language of actions more than words. It demands to be shown, to be felt in gestures that bridge the chasm between two souls. Her love for me was displayed in action. For example I would be thirsty, but not verbalize it. She would come and hand me a glass of cold water. I would be hungry and not say anything, yet she would come and bring me a snack, a bag of potato chips or a Hershey's candy bar that was her love. As I write those words, I am reminded of the scripture in Matthew 25:35-40: *For I was an hungred, and ye gave me meat: I was thirsty, and ye gave me drink: I was a stranger, and ye took me in: Naked, and ye clothed me: I was sick, and ye visited me: I was in prison, and ye came unto me. Then shall the righteous answer him, saying, Lord, when saw we thee an hungred, and fed thee? or thirsty, and gave thee drink? When saw we thee a stranger, and took thee in? or naked, and clothed thee? Or when saw we thee sick, or in prison, and came unto thee? And the King shall answer and say unto them, Verily I say unto you, inasmuch as ye have done it unto one of the least of these my brethren, ye have done it unto me.*

Her love was such that she anticipated my needs and fulfilled them before I was aware that they existed. I pray that I showed her that same love in return. She knew what I needed even when I did not know myself. And yet, I wrestle with whether my actions ever truly spoke the volumes my heart carried. Were my whispered affections, my small offerings of comfort, enough? Or did my love remain suspended in words, unanchored and intangible?

These doubts seep into my soul, haunting me in moments of solitude. I replay every memory, searching for clarity, yet finding only the ache of uncertainty. The weight of her absence transforms these questions into jagged edges. The vows we took, "Until death do us part," now echo with a cruel irony. Words that were once a part of a sacred vow that brought so much joy in the morning now echo the cruel reality of their ultimate meaning. In that instant standing there at the altar the words, "Until death do you part" spoken but yet the ramification of the meanings missed because of the euphoric joy in the moment. The joy of being betrothed to the one you love. Love, once a sanctuary, now feels like a labyrinth where every turn reveals another shadow of pain. The words of the marriage ceremony are now a flashlight shining glaring light into that shadow. The words, "In sickness and in health" forced out of the shadow and into the reality of the cancer she contracted. The words seemingly blasted from a megaphone the truth. The truth is that you knew that this could happen and indeed one day it would happen. Yet, in the euphoric happiness of that moment you settled for that possibility knowing that the days of that happiness would be numbered.

In this darkness only illuminated by words uttered in the past, I am left grappling with questions that dig deep into the fabric of the human experience: Is love worth the pain it inevitably leaves behind? Should we dare to bind ourselves with promises, knowing they will one day be tested by mortality? My answer to these questions is a resounding *Yes*. Love is worth the pain. The 48 years of unparalleled bliss infused by her love is worth the pain that I now endure. For what is the alternative to have never loved and therefore never lost. I consider it better to have loved and lost than never to have loved at all. Yes, we must dare to bind ourselves with promises knowing that the day will come that we will be tested by mortality, for what is life but to live and to love? These thoughts, relentless as they are, often silence all but the rhythm of my breath, an inhale, an exhale, a small reminder that even amidst doubt, life continues. The inhale and exhale far more satisfying when they exude love.

Yet, even as these questions haunt me, there's a quiet whisper within, a defiant hope that despite the pain, love is what gives meaning to the chaos. Without love what would be the meaning of each day. The mundane eight-hour-a-day job seems much more tolerable when one knows that at the end of the day their loved one will be waiting. The heart quickens its beat as it anticipates the reunion with the object of one's affection. Love is what binds us to one another. Love is the catalyst that sparks that symbiotic relationship when I inhale; she exhaled for me. As my heart beats, so her heart beat. As my arms unfold to embrace her, her arms unfold to embrace me, and we envelop each other. Love is what elevates us above the silence of existence. And perhaps, it is in embracing both its beauty and its impermanence that we find our truest selves.

Can clarity and understanding be found in the complexity of love and loss? As I sit with that thought permeating my mind, I am reminded of the words to a song from the musical Annie, with that resolute melody: *"Oh, the sun will come out tomorrow, So you've gotta hang on 'til tomorrow Come what may."* These words, simple and unassuming, hold the key to a promise that feels distant, almost unattainable, amidst the silence of loss. Yet, they reverberate, a persistent echo that refuses to fade. I cannot help but wonder: Will the sun truly come out tomorrow? Will the shadows that shroud my heart fade with the rising sun yielding to clarity and understanding? Will the chaos brought about by her death untangle itself into something I can grasp, something I can hold? Will the simplicity and clarity of the love that I have for her return or will it simply be rationalized into a statement such as, "It is better to have loved and lost than never to have loved at all." After all, isn't that what we are encouraged to do, rationalize? Society encourages us to move on as one person put it return to normalcy. What is normal after the love of your life is gone? There is no normal in my future. For 48 years her love for me was normal and my love for her is normal. There now exists a void where I actively shared my love. This void cannot be filled for now the acts that typify my love cannot be displayed.

Her absence, heavy and unyielding, wraps me in a stillness so profound that it feels as if it will last forever. It mocks the very notion of tomorrow, a cruel reminder of the permanence of death, a permanence that I neither chose nor welcomed. And yet, even in this stillness, there is a faint flicker, fragile as it may be, a glimmer of hope that perhaps tomorrow holds the answers I seek. Perhaps clarity will emerge not from unraveling the complexity of love and loss, but rathe from embracing it in all its layered beauty and pain.

I find myself asking (not for the first time) if things will get better. This question, so universal in its plea, feels uniquely mine in the way it rises, desperate and raw, from the depths of my grief. Will the permanence of her absence ever feel less sharp? Will her memory, instead of stinging with what was lost, begin to bloom as a reminder of what was shared; of what was, for a fleeting moment, eternal in its own right? In the quiet, as I wrestle with these thoughts, I realize that perhaps the sun does not promise answers or resolutions. Perhaps it promises only presence, a tomorrow where my breath still rises and falls, where life persists despite its jagged edges.

Her absence teaches me that redemption is not always found in the clarity of understanding, but in the act of continuing, of daring to step into the light, naked and unafraid even when the darkness feels insurmountable. I am naked in that the love that once was my shield is now gone yet, vulnerable as I am, I rise unafraid because knowing if death comes it means I will be with her. And so, I sit with these questions, my mind a tempest of doubt and hope, waiting for the sun to rise. Waiting for its warmth to remind me that even in the permanence of loss, life goes on. That clarity, perhaps, does not reside in answers but in the quiet resilience of the heart. And as faith begins to stir within me, I feel the faintest glimmer of solace, the kind that promises not a resolution, but the strength to navigate tomorrow. And the sweet refrain of Job's words, "*Naked I came, naked I shall return, blessed be the name of the Lord*" echo in the caverns of my mind, faint but resolute.

Chapter 6:
FAITH AND REDEMPTION

In the labyrinth of loss I have often discovered that spiritual reflections become threads of gold. I label them threads of gold because they become a lifeline, a lifeline that pulls you back from the depths. A lifeline subtle, sometimes barely visible, yet strong enough to bear the weight of me and my sorrow. In moments when tragedy pressed close, when darkness seemed absolute, I have known a peculiar kind of peace, The peace that is described in Philippians 4:7 (KJV): "*And the peace of God, which surpasses all understanding, will guard your hearts and your minds in Christ Jesus.*" A peace that does not arrive by intellectual reckoning, but through the Holy Spirit and the gentle persistence of sacred words echoing in the corridors of my mind. Through the years, it is as if God Himself, foreseeing my grief, offered me comfort before the pain had even arrived. I remember vividly when our oldest daughter, full of promise and youth, returned home from ROTC training at Quantico, only to be overcome by an illness that at first seemed nothing more than passing flu. It was lupus, sudden and relentless. In the months leading up to her passing, I would find myself, in the quietest moments, sometimes in the shower, sometimes alone with my thoughts, hearing the scripture (Job 1:21), "... *The LORD giveth and the LORD taketh away; blessed be the name of the LORD*," repeating, unbidden, in my mind. The words were a pillar, a thread of gold something to hold on to, something to hold on to when the ground fell away. This pattern has repeated itself, marked by the recurrence of grief. Twenty years later, at the loss of my niece to the very same illness, again a verse rose up within me (John 14:1): "*Let not your heart be troubled; ye believe in God, believe also in Me.*" Like a river running through the landscape of sorrow, these words smoothed rough stones and offered quiet assurance, even as my heart struggled to accept what had been lost.

When my mother died in 2020 it was the words, "*I am the way, the truth, and the life: no man cometh unto the Father, but by Me*" (John 14:6), that became my refrain. No matter the depth of my anguish, the scripture would come, gentle and persistent, reminding me that the pain of separation was not the end of the story. Those words became lanterns on the path, illuminating my path just enough for me to take the next step.

But perhaps the most startling visitation of comfort came not in words, but in the song the Holy Ghost had gifted me. During my wife's illness I sang that song while preparing dinner, I sang *"Walk with me, Lord,"* and my wife, resting in the bedroom, called out to ask if I was singing her favorite song. I told her I was, and in that simple exchange, I felt the nearness of God, the presence of love that not even death could erase.

These experiences with scripture repeating itself in my mind, songs emerging unbidden in my soul, have carried me through tragedy. They do not erase the pain, nor do they answer the unanswerable questions. But they offer comfort, a balm for the ache, and a reminder that even in the valley of shadow, I am not alone. I hope, as I share these moments, that others too may find such comfort in the sacred echoes that rise up when we need them most.

The significance of (1 Corinthians 15:55) *"O death, where is thy sting? O grave where is thy victory?"* has always resonated with me, particularly in moments when the finality of death seems overwhelming, such as at the graveside, where these words are so often spoken by ministers as a loved one is laid to rest. On the surface, burial feels so absolute, as if it marks an irrevocable ending. Yet I have always found deep comfort in these very words. Far from signaling an end, they speak of a beginning, an assurance, spoken by Jesus, that death is not our ultimate fate. To me, the question, *"O death, where is thy sting?"* powerfully challenges death's authority over life. It declares that death is stripped of its power, because Jesus promised, *"I go to prepare a place for you; that where I am, there ye may be also. And if I go, I shall come again and receive you unto myself"* *(John 14:3)* In this light, death becomes not a fearsome adversary, but a passage, a vehicle that transports us from this world into another, where we will dwell with Christ. The grave itself loses its grip, for when the earth gives up its dead and the battle is over, the victory is ours, and we shall see our loved ones again in heaven.

There are times in my sorrow when the weight of grief seems to eclipse even the faintest glimmer of hope. In these moments, I feel as if the road ahead is lost to shadow, as though the future itself has crumbled beneath my feet. Yet, it is precisely here, in the deepest valleys, where the meaning of Jesus's sacrifice reaches me most profoundly. His suffering was not only for the redemption of the world, but also a gesture of solidarity with every broken heart. Jesus wept, Jesus bled, Jesus died, He entered fully into the depths of human pain, so that no anguish would be foreign or unseen to Him. When I feel there is no path forward, I remember that He walked before me, carrying the full weight of sorrow, betrayal, and loss, so that I would never be alone in my suffering. His resurrection, the promise that death is not the end, becomes a quiet assurance that despair does not have the final word. Even when I cannot see beyond my grief, I find comfort in knowing that Jesus's sacrifice opened a door to hope that is not dependent on my current feelings or circumstances. It reminds me that this pain, however overwhelming, is cradled in hands that have already borne the greatest burden. And so, even when the future seems unimaginable, I cling to the truth that newness, of life, peace, and the possibility of joy, can still dawn, even after the longest night.

Chapter 7:
TO LIVE OR NOT TO LIVE

There is no explaining it. Some mornings the ache is suffocating, an invisible weight pressing against my chest; the world is both too bright and unbearably empty. Grief is unpredictable, one day a gentle ache, the next a relentless storm. There are some days when the effort to rise above sorrow feels like clawing up the slick, yielding sides of a deep pit. I scramble to find a purpose, desperate for the solidity of hope, only to feel the cold soil crumble beneath my fingers. Each attempt to ascend is met by the subtle, relentless pull of despair the ground collapsing, sliding around my ankles, dragging me downward despite my struggle. The sunlight above is visible, tantalizing, and yet it recedes as I am swallowed again by shadow. The exhaustion of this cycle, the hope that flickers and is snuffed out, leaves me raw and aching. Still, in the very act of reaching upward, however futile it may seem, I find a stubborn ember of determination that refuses to die, even as the darkness presses closer.

The questions surface, unbidden and persistent: Do I want to go on living? Can I? Do I possess the courage, or is it simply endurance, to face another day beneath this burden? Sometimes, it feels as if choice itself is an illusion, each possibility blurred by sorrow. There are no easy answers. These questions carve their silent shapes into my thoughts, echoing in the quiet moments. Sometimes I wonder if anyone has ever truly answered them, or if we all simply stumble forward, hoping for the day when the weight grows lighter, or when some small shaft of light reveals a new way out of the darkness. Is there an answer? I do not know. But the asking itself is its own kind of survival, a testament to the part of me that, even in the throes of despair, still searches for hope, still longs for meaning, still dares to believe that somewhere beyond the ache, life is waiting to be reclaimed.

Chapter 8:
THE POETIC SOUL

Blind

My eyes see, yet I am blind.

I am blind to truth for my

Tongue speaks only lies.

I am blind to death for I have never died.

But most of all I am blind to life

For I have never truly lived.

~ Elliott Norman, Sr (1979)

At first glance, "Blind" is a meditation on paradox: the speaker's eyes function, yet blindness prevails, not of sight, but of spirit and understanding. The poem's short lines and sparse language evoke a sense of quiet resignation, each utterance heavy with introspection. The repetition of "I am blind to . . ." establishes a litany of confessions, as if the speaker is peeling back the layers of self-deception and uncertainty that obscure authentic existence. The speaker's blindness to truth, rooted in their own dishonesty, suggests an inner conflict, a tongue "speaking only lies" that distances them from reality. This line introduces the first major symbol: blindness as self-imposed, a consequence of the choices we make and the narratives we perpetuate. Truth, then, becomes something so easily clouded by habit or fear. The acknowledgment of being "blind to death" because the speaker has "never died" is both literal and existential. It gestures toward the unknowable boundaries separating life from death, and how the living can only speculate about the ultimate end. The poet's refusal to claim understanding of death underscores a humility before life's greatest mystery. But the final, most poignant admission—being "blind to life" for never having "truly lived," strikes at the heart of the poem's meaning.

It is an indictment of a half-lived life, a recognition that mere existence is not enough. To "truly live" requires more than sensation or survival; it demands presence, honesty, vulnerability, a willingness to encounter both pain and joy in their fullness. Throughout, the poem's tone is confessional yet searching. There is no attempt to resolve the paradoxes it presents; instead, it dwells in the uncertainty, mirroring the questions that haunt the narrative: Is it enough to ask, to search, to try? Or is sight only meaningful when paired with the courage to live authentically? This poem resonates deeply with the book's larger themes, the will to endure amidst pain, the hunger for meaning, the fear and hope intertwined in every act of survival.

In revealing blindness not as a physical limitation but as an existential condition, "Blind" becomes a quiet challenge: to pursue truth, to confront mortality, and to seize life's fleeting chances for genuine experience. I believe that the fact Blind was included in the National Poets Anthology is a testament to its quiet power and universal resonance. "Blind" occupies a delicate space within the contemporary canon, inviting readers not just to witness the speaker's confessions, but to reckon with their own moments of unseeing. In a collection meant to showcase the nation's most stirring and vital voices, the poem stands out for its willingness to dwell in ambiguity, a rare courage to embrace uncertainty rather than chase resolution. The anthology becomes, through "Blind," not merely a compendium of poetic achievement but a mirror reflecting our shared longing for clarity and authenticity. It challenges both poets and readers to acknowledge the shadows of self-doubt and the possibility of transformation that lies, always, just beyond easy sight.

Delving into the rich symbolism threaded through the poem reveals just how deeply it is entwined with the book's central themes. Each image and metaphor, the blindness that is not of sight, but of spirit; the confessions that peels back layers of self-deception, echoes the narrative's ongoing search for authenticity, truth, and courage in the face of uncertainty. For example, the image of standing at the altar and professing those words of love words uttered with profound sincerity yet the true meaning of those words such as, "Until death do us part," somehow lost in self-deception for 48 years return now to echo their factual authenticity and truth.

The poem's motifs of seeing and unseeing, of longing and resignation, do not stand alone; they reflect and amplify the book's explorations of survival, regret, and the hunger for meaning. The motif of seeing represented in life by choosing to acknowledge the words, "Do you promise to love cherish and honor . . . " and the motif of unseen represented in life by the deception that, "Until death do you part" is unreal or will never happen. The motif of longing now is my constant companion in her absence. Resignation is an elusive commodity because if I accept things as they are then all hope is gone. The numerous threads That make up the fabric of my existence in real life are echoed in the sentiments of the poem. In this way, the poem becomes not just a solitary meditation, but a vital thread in the tapestry of the book's larger story.

Chapter 9:
THE BURDEN OF REGRET

In hindsight—which presents itself as clear-eyed reckoning with the actions taken, and those left undone, during her last days, I find myself haunted by a litany of doubts and regrets: first, consenting to place her in hospice care. I had always assumed that when someone was placed in hospice it was done to give them better care. One of the things that I did not know about hospice is the fact that if the patient goes into cardiac arrest there will not be any attempt made to resuscitate them. I wanted my wife in hospice so that her suffering would be eased by proper medication and someone being with her at all times to assure that she was comfortable.

I had no idea that placing her in hospice meant that we were giving up, in essence throwing in the towel. I wanted everything possible to be done to ensure that my wife had every opportunity to live not to give up. I must admit that some of my desire for her to be on hospice was born out of selfishness in that I was tired and weary and desperately needed some rest. Having her in hospice meant that there would be someone with her and she would no longer be in pain. In that way I could rest secure in the knowledge that she would be well taken care of. As I watched her lying there quietly, as if asleep, not crying out in pain. As the morphine took effect, I felt that I had done the right thing. She was finally getting some rest after weeks of indescribable agony and pain. Perhaps I can find some consolation in that, perhaps.

Second, speaking candidly about her prognosis with doctors and hospice staff at her bedside, never considering the fact she might hear every word. One of the things that I learned at combat medic school at Fort Sam Houston Texas was that you should always speak only of the positive when treating your patient and that all negative information should be discussed where the patient cannot hear. I don't know why I allowed people to enter the room and stand beside her bed and discuss how far the cancer has spread or how long she had to live. I would like to think that I was off guard or somehow unconscious to what was being said until after it was said. I do remember my mind being in sort of a fog. It was as if I was having an out-of-body experience instead of dealing with the reality of what was happening. My conscience refuses to accept any excuse or rationalization. I did it, I know it was wrong and there's nothing I can do to change it.

Third, discussing funeral home arrangements while she still breathed, not stepping into the hallway for that conversation. That statement isn't exactly correct. It's amazing how when we seek to place blame, we lump things into one neat little package. What actually happened was I was standing beside my wife's hospital bed looking down at her with my hand under my chin. I was in deep contemplation about something, I don't know what, but I remember a voice saying, "Have you guys given any thought to a Funeral Home." As if by reflex, I thought for a moment not breaking my concentration on whatever was on my mind and said in a haphazard manner not making eye contact with my daughter son or son in law, Williams Funeral Home on Tobacco Road? My daughter responded I guess so shrugging her shoulders. The hospice representative repeated Williams Funeral Home? In that instance my concentration was broken, and I realized that I had been standing beside her bed while she was still alive discussing what would happen after her death as if she had already died. The gloom that I felt weighed heavily upon my heart. I felt that I had betrayed her. I felt that I had neglected my faith. In that instance I was guilty, guilty of giving up before the fight was over. One of the things that I realize now is that even if I had not responded the damage would have already been done by the verbalization of the words, "Have you guys given any thought to a funeral home?" The fact that those words were uttered means that they could not be unspoken. So, it makes no difference. Stepping into the hallway to discuss the matter although it may have relieved my conscience somewhat, if my wife heard those words the damage was already done. That does not relieve my guilt however it does shine a light on the true facts and events that occurred.

Fourth, what if I had taken her to the hospital sooner? Would an early hospital visit have saved her life? I can't help but wonder. Was there was anything more I could have done for her? These questions fuel my guilt. However, there is a deeper idea that is uncovered by these questions. The question of ego. Who am I, that I think that I could have somehow impacted on the events that took place that day. I am a Christian. Therefore, I believe that God has all power in his hand. And further, I believe that all things work together for good for those that love the Lord. Yet, with these questions I act as if I have some type of control over life and death as if by some thought or action I could save my wife's life. I prayed constantly for my wife. And I remember her words, "I'm not worried, God's got me!" The nonchalant manner in which she said those words with such sincerity and laid her head back down on her pillow made me love and admire her even more. In the face of all that she was suffering she knew that God would take care of her. I prayed that I would bravely exhibit such faith if I were in here situation.

Finally (and most painful of all) I regret not being present in the hospital at the moment she died. I was at home, our home, sitting in the recliner that she had chosen for me. I can see pictures of the moment in my mind's eye. It was early morning around 7:30 AM. I was chatting with my son. At that moment we both have forgotten the gravity of the situation and our fear that my wife might die. I had come home the night before seeking some rest from the weeks of desperation and fear. In that moment as I said the gravity of our situation seemed a distant memory. However, the ringing of the telephone broke those moments of sweet respite and suddenly we were confronted again with the reality of our desperate situation. My son answered the telephone, and he walked toward me with the telephone, and I could see by his furrowed eyebrows that he was listening intently. I could hear him say OK, thank you.

And in that instant I knew that my wife was dead. My son spoke the words, but I already knew, he said the nurse said Mom died a little after 7:00 this morning. I held my coffee cup to my lips but did not sip. It was as if the aroma of the coffee would awaken me from what I thought was a dream. Somehow deep in the crevices of my mind I did not believe my wife would die. We fought so many battles together and we'd always come through. God brought us through. I thought that no matter how insurmountable the odds of survival in this case with God's help we would again arise triumphant. The thing that I overlooked with that point of view is that in my wife's condition perhaps we did rise triumphantly. With cancer spread to her liver, lungs, spinal column, and brain, what kind of life would she had if she had lived. In my selfishness I think only of my loss. I don't think about how much pain she would have had to endure or what God's purpose is in her death.

These memories gather in my mind, each one a quiet ache that asks, again and again: if I had done anything differently, made other choices, acted sooner, spoken more carefully, would she still be alive? The uncertainty lingers, inviting both anguish and reflection, demanding a difficult kind of honesty with myself. Wrestling with the persistent question: If I had chosen differently, would she still be here? There is exquisite agony in the mind's relentless replay of those pivotal moments, as if their very repetition might yield different answers or soften the ache of uncertainty. The questions return with the constancy of a wave beating against a rock at the seashore: Was it right to speak so openly in her presence? Should I have shielded her from harsh truths, or would that have been a greater betrayal? Each "what if" is a needle, threading through memory's fabric, refusing to let old wounds close. The pain lies not only in the memories themselves, but in their endless rehearsal, an inner interrogation that never quite resolves, yet refuses to quiet.

Wrestling with these questions is to be captive of a kind of private hell, where remorse and longing become indistinguishable. Is the remorse that I experience sorrow because she is dead or me yearning for the loss of all that she meant to me? Is it the natural tendency for one human to empathize with the condition of another or the selfish longing for what once was? Suddenly those familiar words from those precious happy times of early childhood return with newfound vigor, "Once upon a time." It is a cycle of both punishment and strangely hopefulness, as if the mind believes that by sheer persistence, absolution or understanding might at last be found. But each round of questioning seems only to deepen the mystery, and the heart is left holding the same unrelenting ache.

The Challenge of Acceptance

- The Weight of "What-if": One of the greatest obstacles to making peace with immutable outcomes is the mind's relentless return to the past, those endless cycles of "what if." These questions, though unanswerable, persist in replaying alternative scenarios, each one a new avenue for regret. The desire to rewrite difficult chapters is both deeply human and quietly punishing, often stalling the journey toward acceptance.

- Self-Blame and Guilt: When reflecting on actions taken or opportunities missed, guilt can settle in like a fog. The sense of responsibility no matter how disproportionate, may overshadow objective reality, making it difficult to grant oneself forgiveness or grace. Untangling genuine accountability from the burdensome weight of self-blame becomes a delicate, ongoing task.

- The Hunger for Closure: Accepting what cannot be changed often means relinquishing the hope for tidy closure. There are rarely satisfying answers or dramatic resolutions; instead, one learns to live with loose ends and silent questions. This ambiguity challenges the need for certainty and sometimes leaves an ache that must be tended with patience.

- Letting Go of Control: At the core, making peace is an act of surrender, a recognition of both the limits of our power and the unpredictability of life. Releasing the illusion that every outcome was within our grasp can feel like giving up, when in truth, it is an act of profound courage and humility.

- Finding Meaning in the Unchangeable: Ultimately, the path to peace may require reframing loss and regret as teachers rather than punishments. This means seeking meaning in pain, allowing wounds to foster empathy, and discovering new layers of self-understanding. It is a gradual process, one measured not in days or accomplishments, but in the quiet work of the heart.

Chapter 10:
CONVERSATIONS UNHEARD

Did she overhear us speaking in those hushed, anxious tones? Did the mention of arrangements, the unthinkable logistics, somehow reach her even in sedation, echo in the quiet aftermath, haunting the corridors of memory. Science offers little certainty about the boundaries of awareness in such states. Yet, there remains a lingering intuition that consciousness is not always confined by the visible signs of wakefulness. Perhaps, on some level only the heart can sense, she registered our words—the tremor in a voice, the weight of our silences, maybe even the heartbreak behind the practicalities we tried so hard to shield from her.

We ask ourselves if she was aware, even as her breathing grew shallow, of the gravity in the room when we first spoke, faltering, about what might happen next. Did she feel us wrestling with impossible decisions, and did some part of her spirit take comfort, or pain, from what was said or left unsaid? These are the mysteries we carry: whether, in those suspended hours, she lingered between our world and another, attuned to the love and fear threaded through every gesture, every word. And so, we continue, uncertain, left to ponder the porous boundary between the spoken and the unheard, the waking and the unconscious. It becomes part of the quiet sorrow, and also perhaps a fragile hope, that somehow, she knew she was surrounded by care, even when we believed her unaware.

Communication during times of grief is a double-edged sword, it is essential for those navigating loss, yet it is fraught with unforeseen consequences. Words spoken at the bedside, out of earshot (or so we hope) may reach further than we intend. What if she did hear us? What if our anxious conversations and whispered logistics meant to shield her, instead slipped through the haze and found their way to her heart? The possibility is unsettling. On one hand, hearing our voices, tremulous with love and worry, might have brought comfort, a silent affirmation that she was not alone, that every decision was made with care and devotion. Yet, there is the counterweight of fear: that the weight of our uncertainty, the sorrow stitched into our practicalities, may have signaled a loss of hope, perhaps even nudged her spirit toward surrender.

Did our words help her hold on, or did they make letting go feel inevitable? The truth remains obscured, suspended between the boundaries of consciousness and unawareness. In these moments, we are left wrestling not only with grief but also with the imponderable effect our communication may have had, wondering if, despite our well-meaning intentions, we inadvertently contributed to the ebbing of her will. Ultimately, these questions are threads in the tapestry of mourning: reminders of how even the gentlest communication can ripple outward, beyond our reach, shaping both our own healing and the journey of those we love.

Learning to forgive oneself for perceived missteps is a journey marked by tenderness and courage. It begins in the quiet reckoning with our own humanity, a recognition that to be alive is to be imperfect, to care is to be vulnerable. The mind replays moments of uncertainty, words said or left unsaid, actions taken or hesitated over, and we find ourselves questioning not only what we did, but who we are. Self-forgiveness does not arrive all at once. It grows slowly, watered by honest reflection and gentle acceptance that, in love and loss, the heart will sometimes falter. The brain forgets what it knows. We must first acknowledge our pain, the wish that we could have done otherwise, and the fact that we are not in control. We are mere mortals limited by the fact that we are mortal, imperfect, flawed, faulty, defective, unsalable, inferior, substandard and characterized by our propensity to make mistakes. Once we acknowledge these facts then, with time, we learn to speak inwardly as we would to a dear friend, offering kindness instead of condemnation, understanding instead of shame.

This process encourages us to disentangle intention from outcome, to recognize that our choices were shaped by the knowledge and emotion we possessed in those singular, unrepeatable moments. We must acknowledge that our perception that we could impact an outcome is just another attempt by our ego to bolster our self-importance. Everything isn't about me. We look for the lessons amid sorrow, and in doing so, find the beginnings of grace: the realization that growth is not measured by perfection, but by the willingness to realize our limitations and acknowledge God's omnipotence. Forgiving oneself is not to erase what happened or to ignore its impact, but to allow the heart to soften around the ache, to give ourselves permission to heal. In the gentle light of self-compassion, we gradually release the heavy mantle of regret, making room for new beginnings, and for the quiet confidence that, despite our flaws, we are still deserving of peace. I am reminded of Jesus' words in John 14:27: *"Peace I leave with you, my peace I give unto you: not as the world giveth, give I unto you. Let not your heart be troubled, neither let it be afraid."*

Chapter 11:
THE COUNSELOR'S TRUTH

When we first sat with the doctor at the Oncology Center, still reeling from the shock of an emergency room diagnosis, metastatic cancer, there was a glimmer of hope offered: the cancer, though aggressive, might also be more responsive to treatment. The doctor's exact words were, "This is an aggressive cancer, it spreads fast, but it can be killed easily." We clung to this, believing in the possibility of a swift and positive outcome. In those early months, the transformation felt miraculous. My wife, who had arrived in a wheelchair, unable to manage even the simplest tasks, gradually regained her strength. By October, she was walking independently again, cooking, tidying, and making the bed each morning. It was a testament, it seemed, to the promise of recovery.

But hope is fragile. By January, the optimism we'd nurtured faltered. The new plan was maintenance therapy, and after her first infusion, everything changed. She grew ill almost immediately, and within two weeks, she was back in the wheelchair, unable to stand without help. The doctor acknowledged the treatment wasn't working and said we would try something else, but before the new regimen could begin, she slipped away from us.

Throughout those months, the advice from nurses and technicians echoed in my mind: "Just do the best you can." Those words (though uttered innocently) at the time, now seem like ominous precursors of what was to come. I tried, gathering specimens for labs and managing the daily routines of care. Now in the aftermath I wonder, did I really do my best? Could I have done more, or could I have done things differently? These questions linger, persistent and unanswerable, intertwined with the wisdom and limitations imparted by counselors and medical staff. They become part of the ongoing self-examination that accompanies loss, a quiet search for meaning amid the unchangeable past.

I have always been what psychology might call an overactive achiever, not because I possess any extraordinary intelligence, but because of something more steadfast: tenacity. Like a bulldog, once I set my mind to a commitment, I hold on until either the task is done, or I have simply exhausted every option. This quality, tenacity, has defined much of my life. When it came to caring for my wife during her illness, I approached that responsibility with the same unwavering resolve. Whether in managing her care, advocating for her, or praying with her in the quiet hours, I felt this duty belonged to me alone. I took my wedding vows seriously, "To love, honor, and cherish, in sickness and in health, until death do us part", and I meant every word. Yet, when the outcome was not what I had so fiercely hoped for, I found myself grappling with some of the same difficult questions repeatedly. Did I truly do my best? Where did I fall short? Is acknowledging my mistakes the same as accepting failure? Or is it a recognition of my humanity, a humble admission that, despite all efforts and intentions, we are all bound by our limitations?

In seeking balance, I remind myself that responsibility and acceptance are not adversaries. To accept that I did what I could is not to excuse myself from the pain of loss or the wish that things had been different. Rather, it's to honor the love that fueled my efforts and to grant myself the same compassion I would offer to anyone else: that doing one's best is, in the end, all any of us can do. In this space between tenacity and humility, I continue to learn what it truly means to care, to endure, and, ultimately, to forgive myself.

During my wife's illness, I spent long periods of time gazing into my reflection, searching for answers in the lines and shadows of my own face. The mirror did not flatter. It showed my faults with startling honesty. I was frightened, uncertain, and deeply lost. My blemishes stood out, like a banana whose peel still clings but whose bruised spots reveal the tender injuries beneath. Every feature I'd learned to dislike about myself seemed magnified, from the stubborn curl in the center of my scalp that never lies flat, a small defiance that has persisted since my birth, to the marks and scars that map my years. With all these imperfections, I began to wonder: is there any grace for someone like me?

The idea of grace, as described in the Bible, is God's unearned favor and boundless love poured out upon humanity. But does that really include me? With all my flaws and failings, am I truly worthy of receiving God's grace? These are the questions I carry, quietly and continually, as I move through each day. And slowly, as I face myself, imperfections, fears, and all. I begin to realize that grace is not earned by perfection. Rather, it is offered freely, even, and perhaps especially, to those of us who feel most bruised and broken. In this realization, I find a tender hope that, despite everything, I am held in a love that sees beyond my flaws and welcomes me, just as I am.

Epilogue

"Goodnight, I'll see you in the morning." Words of childhood dreams and endless possibilities. Words that represent a universal connection between humanity. Words that are spoken to children as their parents put them to bed the same words that follow these words said in unison by parents and children: *Now I lay me down to sleep, I pray the Lord my soul to keep, if I should die before I wake I pray the Lord my soul to take.* The same words are spoken to each other by husband and wife after the workday has ended, and the children are safely tucked into their beds. The words which in the past have brought me comfort are now the source of my survivor's remorse. My initiation to death and grief in the glove box of an old Studebaker, educated me, but it seemed an abstract concept for a five-year-old. When my grandmother died, I realized that grief had been a stranger to me, an abstract concept. But with her death my education was complete death was real not an abstract concept. Death was accompanied by grief which I fought alone.

Like sand through an hourglass the years waxed on, and God gave me a helpmate. The love of my life, Lady Di. I never had to fight alone again. She was there for me. She stands with me through every battle including this, once, stranger. Our love for each other shaped the days of our lives. In times when the weight of the grief from the death of a loved one threatened to pull us under, we found strength in each other's arms and in our shared vulnerability. Our strength lies in our willingness to reach for each other's hands, and in our quiet promise to carry on together. Our strength was our love for each other. My strength is my love for her.

The words of this book exemplify my search for redemption after her death. I search for redemption because I find myself haunted by a litany of doubts and regrets about what I did and did not do. The path to peace requires reframing loss and regret; they become teachers rather than punishments. Also, understanding my pain, allowing wounds to foster empathy, and uncovering facts that are omitted when I allow grief to guide my thoughts. It is a gradual process, one measured not in days or accomplishments, but in the quiet work of the heart. I feel that I have found the catalyst for my redemption. The catalyst for redemption is so simple that I am not surprised that I overlooked it. The catalyst can be found in these words of 1 Corinthians `13:13 (KJV): *"And now abideth faith, hope, charity, these three; but the greatest of these is charity."* Charity is love. My redemption lies in her love for me. As I said earlier, love in its purest form, has the power to define us, to shape us into beings capable of profound joy and profound sorrow.

Her love defined and shaped me by changing me from the hard shell that I was and shaping me into a being who could express love for others. The threads of her existence sutured the lacerations deep in my soul, thus piercing my hard shell. My life, broken as it was, was mended by her gentle touch. The words, "I love you" now spring effortlessly from lips that once held them captive. Her love, my redemption, allows me to dare to step into the light, naked and unafraid even when the darkness feels insurmountable. I can go on.

"Good night, I'll see you In the Morning" is not an ending, but a new beginning for us. I Love You!

AUTHOR'S BIOGRAPHY

Rev. Elliott S. Norman Sr. holds a BA in Sociology and Social Work from Augusta College, and a Master of Arts in Biblical Counseling from Luther Rice Seminary. Rev. Norman began his kindergarten and elementary school education in Barcelona Spain where he attended an all-Spanish speaking Catholic school in the late 1950's. Reverend Norman served as a Combat Medic in the United States Army; he also worked at the United Church of Christ headquarters in New York City. Reverend Norman retired from the Department of Juvenile Justice for the State of Georgia where he worked as a social worker and a drug and alcohol counselor. Rev. Norman asserts that without God he can do nothing.